Inside Out Home Automation!

Inside Out Home Automation!

Home Made Power Plant

Discover How To Pay Only $3 For Electricity This Month... Next Month... Forever...

Discover The Naked Truth about Alternative Electricity!

 Save hundreds of dollars (even thousands) in electricity bill each month without lifting a finger.

 Earn a "fat" check every month from the power company for the extra electricity you produce.

 Extremely easy & cheap to build your own solar & wind generators (Approx. $200 investment and it will last a lifetime)

 Fully illustrated manual, and it is explained in plain English so even the least mechanically inclined person can understand and implement the ideas.

 Have a significant role in saving the planet because you'll be one of the pioneers who will help eradicate the huge deposits of CO_2 killing our planet.

 Claim Your Copy "HomeMadePowerPlant"

Use Water As Fuel!

Do you want to know RIGHT NOW how YOU can drive around using WATER AS FUEL and LAUGH at RISING GAS COSTS... while REDUCING emissions and help PREVENT GLOBAL WARMING?

While 100% "water cars" and "water trucks" are still on the drawing board, I am very excited to show you how you can start RIGHT NOW and use Water4Gas to...Convert Your Car/Truck to BURN WATER as well as Gasoline and BOOST YOUR GAS MILEAGE!!!

Inside Out Home Automation!

Contents

What Is Home Automation? 8
The Benefits Of Home Automation 9
Methods Of Home Automation Control 11
Just What Is X10 Technology? 13
Building An Automated Home 14
What Home Automation Can Do for Your Family and Home 16
Home Automation: Providing Your Extra Comfort And Convenience In Your Daily Life ... 19
Smart House Atlanta, The Answer To Home Automation 21
Home Automation Business, Light Dimming Systems Works Wonder 24
Home Automation, Let The Latest Technology Controls Your Home 27
Home Automation And The Mile-High City Of Denver 29
The History Of Home Automation Inc 31
Home Automation Jobs In Florida 34
How Automation Software, Automating Your House 36
Home Automation System, How It Works And What It Means For Your Life 38
Linux Home Automation Systems, Controlling Your Home Through Linux 40
Stanley Home Automation System, A Great Product For Your Everyday Needs 42
Streamingmedia, Knowing The Latest News About Home Automation Systems 44
Wireless Home Automation, What This Means For Your Daily Life 46
The Home Automation Code 48
Home Automation Gear 51
Do-it-Yourself Home Automation Projects 54
GE Products For Home Automation Security And Protection 56
Home Automation And GE Products For Excellent Lighting And Security 58
Advantages Of Home Automation Systems 60
Home Automation Through Voice Recognition Systems 62
Home Automation For Light Control 64
Security CHS 400 Home Automation System 66
Streaming Media In Home Automation 68
Avenues Of Home Automation - Future Living, An Insight 70

What Is Home Automation?

As a very basic definition of home automation you could consider it to be anything that is able to be controlled in your home. If you have a remote or you have automatic control over the function within your home, you have home automation. Today's standards are high. There are actually a number of different ways that you can install this type of automation into your home, which you will see in later chapters.

What's important to know is that most of the automation that you will do will not require hard work. It won't require tearing apart your home or spending thousands of dollars on a simple system. Home automation is something that the average person can do. Most of the products that you will find are simple to install and they don't have to be more than a few hours worth of a project.

Home automation can allow you, and your computer, to make the things that you need and do in your home easier to accomplish. Perhaps you want to control your security system? Or, perhaps you want to voice automate the lights in your home so that you can get into bed and then turn the lights out. Or, perhaps you want to be able to control your sound system from anyplace in your home.

No matter what it is you are looking to accomplish, home automation products are probably available to help you to make it happen.

The Benefits Of Home Automation

The reason that many of the home automation products have been developed is that of convenience. People love being lazy, and in short, that's just fine when it comes to automation options.

Do you remember when you were younger not having a remote control for the television. Yes, there was a time when you actually did have to get up to turn the channels. As difficult as that was, the television remote was one of the first automation tools and by far one of the most used automation tools today.

Convenience with home automation goes farther than this, though. You'll gain the ability to do more, faster and easier. For example, you can heat your home, run a bath, dim the lights, warm your bed before you make it up the stairs and so much more. A popular choice is that of the bathroom and shower models which will actually get your bathroom heater and shower running five minutes before your alarm clock goes off to wake you up. Yes, no more cold showers and cold bathroom floors!

Convenience is the reason most people do turn to home automation and even why some businesses are using it for their needs, too. What things do you do daily that you would love to avoid? What short cuts would make your life a bit better, even if just minimally?

Although convenience may be why you are considering using home automation, there is likely to be some safety benefits available to you as well. Depending on the types of products that you purchase, you can secure your home, with or without the help of an alarm system.

Consider the options. To help protect your home from predators, you can secure motion detecting lights to surround your home. Not only will they turn on when they detect any type of movement in an area where there shouldn't be, but they can alert you to this, too.

You can set it up to alert you with an email to your work account or you can have an automated recording call you to alert you.

Home Automation Inside Out!

If you work nights or don't like coming home to a dark house, you can configure your lighting system to turn on as you are approaching. Even from down the street, your home is well light, comfortable and there's no way anything is lurking in the shadows without your knowledge of it.

Safety is important inside the home as well. If there is something that's gone wrong and there's water in the basement, an alert can be sent to you. Or, if the temperature of the home falls to a certain level, that too can be alerted to you. Home automation really puts you in charge of your home's safety. Without much cost and much trouble, you can set up your home to be safe from the moment you get up to the moment you fall asleep and beyond.

Methods Of Home Automation Control

This is where home automation gets a bit technical, but even still it's easy to understand and it couldn't be easier to install into your home. But, when you get out there and start looking at products to help automate you home's systems, you'll want to take into consider several of these methods. Some may work better for you than others.

These methods also help to define the cost of the product too. Remember, you can automate much of your home inexpensively. But, there is a different level of automation available in the various types of tools available. Learning more about each of these will help you to make the right decision for the product that's out there for you.

Take a few minutes to compare the different methods of controlling your home automation. Select the one that seems to fit your lifestyle, your needs and your budget the best.

Most home automation is controlled using some type of remote. Just like turning on your television or DVD player, using a remote makes life easier.
In home automation, you'll have one remote (generally) that allows you to control the types of automation that are available in that home. If you've installed kits for automation within your home, you'll have a remote to activate and use them as you see fit.

In home automation, your remote control will provide you with the power to control your lights, your security system, your irrigation system, and your appliances. Many of these remotes work throughout the home, even from the other end of the room.

Infrared technology is commonly used with home automation. The remote control options are one of the most affordable choices, and therefore are often used for the smallest budgets. You'll find that they start at just $10 and move up, depending on what they are designed for.

Infrared does have the disadvantage of requiring a "line of sight" style of remote control. You'll have to point the remote at the application, appliance or device for it to make any changes happen.

Home Automation Inside Out!

You'll find that Infrared is used in many television remote controls as well as other consumer style electronics and appliances. Most of the remote controls you pick up today will have this type of technology in them.

You want to set up your Christmas lights to come on at dusk and to turn off at ten. You would want to use automatic technology to make that happen, so you don't have to actually get out there and point a remote to them.

Lighting is heavily done with automatic control both indoor and outdoor. Other appliances can also have this feature including thermostats, security systems and heating units. 43
Included in automatic control is the ability to press one button on your remote and get several functions accomplished by it.

Just What Is X10 Technology?

One of the most popular types of technology for home automation is that of X10. There are many brands of product on the market that you can use, and by no means is this e-book saying that X10 is the best. But, it is one of the most popular and the most likely that you'll begin using. For that reason, you should look into the benefits that it can offer and understand what it means to use these products in your home.

X10 is a type of communication. It's the language that your devices are talking with and therefore doing the things that you ask them to do. It's what makes the two products compatible. Consider it the translator between two people that speak different languages. Without it, automation simply can't work because the units can't tell the other way to do. X10 uses the electrical outlets and wiring devices that you already have set up in your home. This means that you don't have to tear down walls to get the benefits that it can offer to you as you would if you were to hardwire the devices to work

Of course, not having to use hardwire devices means that the product is also quite affordable to use. The actual purchase of X10 products is also affordable. The combination of these two elements makes X10 so important to the world of home automation. Installing this communication tool in your home is simple. You simply need to install the transmitter, which plugs right into outlet in your wall and sends out a control signal to the device. The device is plugged right into a receiver and then into the wall.

When the device receives a signal from the receiver that the transmitter is sending, it performs the task that's being asked of it. Really, it's pretty simple to understand. You can program your X10 units with one of up to 256 different addresses. The address identifies which product is to be used to make the change that you are requesting.

Using this technology, you can also assign two products with the same address so that you can turn them on or off at the same time. This allows you the ability to control many units at once, if that's what you need and want to do with your X10 product. The good thing about X10, in addition to these things, is that all X10 products can be matched together. No matter the brand name, you can mix them together to get the desired effect.

Building An Automated Home

Did you know that the expectation by many was that when home automation technology came onto the market it would be so beneficial and life changing that it would be installed in virtually every home quickly?

But, there are many things that left it in the dust, including an overrun imagination that many had. From the "Jetson's" style of cartoon, many believed that automating the home was going to be a way to let robots handle virtually all aspects of our days. That didn't quite make it, or at least hasn't to this point. The fact that it hasn't reached that level yet has frustrated some, but for others it just means another far researching goal is set.

Yet, do homes have to be so far behind in this technology? Why can't you have all of the home automation that you crave? You can, but in most cases, there is a rather steep cost that must be paid to make it actually happen in your home for you.

The cost of rewiring a home and tearing up the walls to install a home automation tool isn't something that you are likely to do. In fact, it could cost you some serious investment to do this throughout your home. For that reason, many have decided not to install such life altering home automation tools.

Good or bad, that's what happened. Yet, if you are building a new home, things have changed considerably and for that there are many opportunities for success and well being.

If you are building your own home, there is no reason not to consider home automation as part of it. Because the walls aren't yet set up, you can make many changes that can help to lay the foundation for a home that's completely automated. It is essential to know what goes into these home building projects, though. You will need to work with a competent builder who will guide you through the process giving you step by step direction to take.

Even still, it's important to consider these points about home automation and the building of your home.

Home Automation Inside Out!

When building your automated home, the first things you need to take into consideration are your needs. If you visit an online retailer offering home automation products, you'll have an easy time of choosing the right ones for you. In fact, you may just want to install one of each into your home's design.

As part of the building process, you should consider your future needs in regards to home automation. What do you want now and what could you want later? Remember, it is easy to add these affordable differences into your home when the walls are still going up! That's not true when they are coming down!

You will want to develop a proposal that includes all of the pre wiring and home automation projects to your builder. You'll want to work on the electrical plans first and foremost because these will be vitally important to your automation system's success from the start.

By working out what you would like and how it effects the home's wiring needs, you can easily get your home on the right track.

What Home Automation Can Do for Your Family and Home

It's quite amazing to see movies that feature automated devices. They seem impossible to have in this real world. But it's not all camera tricks. Because of today's highly advanced technology, automated devices and gadgets are now possible. You can even have it in your own home.

Home automation is now widely available especially in wealthy countries. People who have it in their homes say that it's part of the house, like outdoor and indoor decorations. These home automation gadgets may be very important to some people, but there are also those who regard it as a waste of money or just a silly device.

Different people have different needs and uses for home automation gadgets. If you have a habit of buying things that are not useful, then it would be better to invest on HA. Home automation is divided into categories, the first one is security and the other one is convenience.

Security

Regular alarm systems are not very popular these days. That is why with home automation, the alarm systems now have built-in HA features. With the old models of alarm systems, they only make a sound after a burglar broke into the house. This gives the burglar time to ransack your home and escape even before authorities get there.

If you're using automated alarm systems, you don't have to lurch half-naked at night looking for the burglar. You will simply push a button, probably located on your bed's side, to turn the lights on. Or your alarm system automatically turns on the light when an intruder enters your premises.

With HA alarms, you're adding anticipation of a possible break-in in your homes. With good lighting, crime can be prevented. Even police authorities agree to that fact. You don't have to change your porch light or any other light in your home. You simply add the gadget, and there you have it, a home safe from burglars, vandals, and trespassers.

Home Automation Inside Out!

Most traditional alarms are primarily designed to protect your property, but not you. But if you utilize HA, you can have control over the whole situation. Personal safety is greatly achieved through home automation. Aside from protecting your property, you also help protect yourself and your family members from injuries like tripping over/falling down the stairs. One switch is enough, and you're guaranteed with utmost security.

Convenience

Who wouldn't want to experience convenience; with today's technology, that is the greatest advantage that you're sure to get. With home automation, everything is done with just one switch.

For many years, you have been used to walking to and fro inside your home turning on the light, checking locks on doors and windows, or turning the heat switch on after waking in the morning. With HA, you don't have to argue who's going to do it. In fact, every one in the house will be glad to press that switch. But having this much convenience is not a valid excuse for you to become a couch-potato.

Having HA around is quite neat and elegant. With a remote control or switch, you can turn on the television, the lights, the VCR, and many more.

If you want to get automated, you just have to set it up. Ask for professional help because there are hundreds of devices compatible with other pieces that can be put together. Getting your home automated can help you solve vast problems that have been there for years.

Home automation can improve a person's life. Learn about HA products through application books and through the internet. Afterwards, you can buy these devices; you may want to stick with DIY gadgets so that you don't have to pay for professional service fees.

You should first identify what particular area(s) in the house that you want HA placed, and call a reputable HA company and ask for help in selecting the appropriate devices.

Home Automation Inside Out!

The best person to know what HA can do for your family and home is you. If you think only electronic geniuses can use HA, you're quite wrong. Seek the help of professionals and enjoy the benefits of home automation.

Investing on HA can be rewarding although the payback time is rather long. But you can't put your family's life at stake; so get your home automated.

Home Automation: Providing Your Extra Comfort And Convenience In Your Daily Life

It is a fact that people today are finding new ways to make their lives a little easier to live. Some people even purchase home spa equipments in order to relax more at the comforts of their own home. Home entertainment systems are also purchased by people in order to relieve stress and hardships they went through in their daily lives.

So, if you have all these features inside your home, you can definitely relax and live your life easier and more comfortable. However, many people are now taking advantage of a new technology that is now widely available in the market today. This technology can and will definitely enhance the way you live your life. With this technology, your daily life will be a lot easier than ever before.

This technology is called home automation systems. As the name suggests, every electronic devices in your home will be automated. You will be able to control every electronic device in your home, such as air conditioners, heaters, home entertainment systems, electronic window blinds, electric ovens, microwave, lights, and even your coffee maker.

Through a control panel, you can control your home anywhere you are. For example, if you are enjoying your favorite movie in your entertainment room, and you forgot to turn on the lights outside your home, you can simply turn it on through your wireless touch screen control panel. This means that you will no longer get up and interrupt your movie to go and switch on the lights.

Another great thing about home automation systems is that most home automations available today are now connected to the internet for remote access. Even when you are out in the office, you can control various electronic devices in your home by accessing a secure website. The great thing about this is that before you go home after a long day at work, you can have everything ready once you get home. You can switch on your stereo system to play your favorite CD, your air conditioning unit, the front porch lights, the garage lights, kitchen lights and even switch on your coffee maker if you want coffee ready for you once you get home.

Home Automation Inside Out!

This means that you will no longer worry about forgetting switching on something inside your home once you are already in your office, such as your home alarm system. For instance, when you are already parked in front of your office, you suddenly remembered that you didn't switch on your home security system, upon reaching the office, you access your home via the internet or through your PDA and easily turn on your home security system.

Some home automation systems are already equipped with security devices, such as CCTV cameras. This means that you can take a look inside and outside your home whenever you want with the internet.

You can even time specific electronic devices to automatically switch on or off at a specified day and at a specified time. This means more convenience and also more security in your home. This is because when you leave on vacation, you can make your home look as if it's inhabited with lights switching on and off at a random pattern everyday. You have to consider that burglars will less likely enter a home that is inhabited. With this kind of system, you can be sure that burglars will think twice before entering your home.

Home automation systems have existed for quite a while now. However, today's home automation systems are much more reliable and also much better than its predecessor.
As you can see, home automation systems are very convenient tools that you should have in your home. Not only that it will make your daily activities a lot easier than before, but it will also provide additional security inside your home.

So, if you want home automation systems installed in your home, you should contact home automation systems installer in your area. Make sure that they can provide you with the best home automation devices by checking the latest home automation technology in tech magazines and on the internet. You should also consult people who have the home automation systems in their home and ask if they are satisfied with it and also ask about the different features and packages available.

Smart House Atlanta, The Answer To Home Automation

You can find businesses anywhere you go. Even in the most remote places, there are still existing businesses big or small. This is because people want to earn money, and they want to provide their customers with useful products or services.

There are many products and services to choose from; and people select only the ones that will be useful in their everyday life. Sometimes, the reason why people can't afford to buy products/services is because of the cost. And when you're talking about home automation, very few people can afford it.

Home automation can make your life at home very comfortable. This is one of the best things offered by advanced technology; and it's just sad to note that not all families can enjoy its benefits. But then again, who knows... the future of fully home automated homes will be a reality to the whole world.

Because of the increasing awareness of this new technology, many home automation companies are making their products more affordable to the public without sacrificing quality, of course. Home automation can bring a new spark to your lighting, HVAC, security systems, and so much more. If you live in Atlanta Georgia, there is one trusted company that provide all your home automation needs, and that is Smart House Digital Interiors. This is the leading supplier of home automation gadgets and devices in Georgia.

Smart House Digital Interiors caters to homeowners, whether it's a new home or you're just remodeling it. You name it, and Digital Interiors can provide it.

They specialize in automation, entertainment, structured wiring, communications, security, and service support. Under home automation, they provide lighting control, energy management, and system integration. They design, install, and service networked systems at home.

If you have a networked electronics system at home, you'll find it reliable, simple to use and it can perform daily functions when triggered by a certain action or it can also be done automatically.

Home Automation Inside Out!

This company is dedicated to use home technology to the fullest by integrating a system for lighting, security, heating, cooling, and other systems to work together. They can guide you from the start of your home automation project until you complete it. They ensure total quality and satisfaction for their customers, and that's what makes them the leading company in Atlanta.

Their secret is to pay attention to all your needs with regards to design, the installation, and proper scheduling. This way, their job is correctly done on time and the result looks very good.

Smart House offers automation packages to make your family's life easy, secure, and comfortable. Aside from that, they guarantee that you'll have a beautiful home and you can save a lot of energy.

Having an automated home in Atlanta is very convenient especially if you're a busy individual. The whole system becomes your active partner in managing your homes.

Smart House's home systems offer a number of features

- automatic activation of security systems during weekdays
- turn lights on/off during the day and night
- lighting scenes are pre-determined and activates automatically
- thermostats are adjusted automatically
- through your telephone, you can check the operation of the system
- touch screens and automation keypads serves as a centralized control on lighting, HVAC, and security

Another important feature of home automation is security. Smart House's security system goes beyond the traditional security systems. The system can detect smoke circuit malfunction, informs you if the alarm is disarmed, has a sleep mode at night to detect extra motion, can be integrated with your HVAC or the lights when you're away. You will be provided with a front door and back yard camera. Some packages provide a baby camera and a pool camera.

Before visiting the store or their online site, you must identify first what things inside your home needs automation. Usually, this decision is based on your allotted budget. But since Smart

Home Automation Inside Out!

House offers automation packages, you can easily choose a package that will suit your budget and your needs.

You'll want to come and stay at home especially if you've already incorporated home automation. Spending quality time with your family will be more memorable if you live in a house of the future.

Home Automation Business, Light Dimming Systems Works Wonder

In the past decades, home automation is considered as a trend of the elites. Today, the need for home automation is very common. Home automation business are simple terms which defines something that gives home owners automatic or remote control operation over their electronic devices at home. Controlling also means interfacing these electronic systems into your laptop or mobile phones. You can control simple things such as security systems, lights, or other related devices. It is all about smart innovation.

There are advantages why people need to incorporate home automation in their daily business.

1. **Convenience.** It provides ease and comfort on the user. Take for instance; through your mobile interfacing system, you can cool your bedroom before you arrive home, setting it to cool at a specified temperature.

2. **Create sophisticated impression.** Any home user would be proud in showing off such technological breakthrough in their home. Combining security systems at your home and controlling other systems using remote control operation is another part of home automation. Controlling fans, air-conditions, lights and others is the most important business for homeowners.

A typical example includes dimming lights to create different moods or scenes. It adds elegance to your room ambiance creating amazing light effects matched with your existing home lights. Enhancing your interiors is not a problem anymore. You will not concentrate more on changing your furniture instead you simply use dimming system in highlighting the living room.

Dimming any kinds of lights such as neon lamps, halogen lamps, fluorescent lamps, and incandescent lamps can be done. However compact fluorescent lamps requires outside dimmable ballast but lamps like metal halide cannot be dimmed. Any residential living room can adapt different functions anytime of the day or night. By just changing light intensities, it can create a scene making the spaces in your living room look great. The great lighting secret lies on how you control it. Lights setting can be saved or retrieved automatically by pressing the right button. You can also delay its time settings for saving two scenes.

Light dimming systems provides the following advantages.

- **Mood lighting.** Light controls can be done to obtain the kind of light you wanted according to its appropriate quantity reducing eyestrain and saving excessive lights.

- **Increases the lifespan of the lamp and saves energy.** It enhances the life of lighting fixtures such as incandescent and halogen. Dimming lights can help you save electricity.

- **Easy installation.** Cabling and time are reduced upon its installations while saving energy. Lighting fixtures switches are eliminated. Qualified electricians can install light dimming systems.

- **Add to your extraordinary interiors.** It enhances interiors and beautifies the space letting selective visuals creates beautiful effects.

- **Convenient.** It is user friendly through a remote control operation or interfaced operation.

The concept of light dimming seem simple to most people. But, it may not always appear like that. It is not just a mere replacement of wall switch thus it can be more complex. Today, day dimming using the latest dimmable ballasts can be no longer easy. Incandescent lamps can be dimmed when voltages are lower. As the voltage decreases, lamp lumens and powers decrease accordingly. The human eyes see a dimmer or brighter light based on the on-time to off-time proportions. It means that 240 is still the actual voltage but its average voltage is already reduced. The phases of cut dimming are categorized into two types.

a. Forward phase cut dimming only energizes the lamps during the final half-cycle portion of the power line. It is cheap and uses tough electronics suitable for many loads.

b.   Reverse phase energizes the lamp during the initial half-cycle portion of the power line. It is more expensive because of using complex electronics. However it is much better on some loads and operates better making less audible sound.

The dimming principle is patterned on how the dimmers work. Generally, dimmers are either thyristors or Triacs. These are utilized for inductive or resistive loads such as cold cathode, low voltage, and incandescent lamp sources. The digital or analog method can also be used for dimming lights depending on the load and application used. Light dimmers can really work wonders in your home.

Home Automation, Let The Latest Technology Controls Your Home

Today's technological breakthrough offers a lot in terms of home devices, home appliances, electronic gadgets, and technological equipments. Although computers or robots are not there to perform household chores like washing plates or cooking dinner, home automation systems will help you in doing these tasks easily and comfortably. Home automation can also provide entertainment while making every task lighter.

The technology today can make everything possible from turning on air conditioners or heaters, recording favorite television shows from any part of the world, or panning surveillance cameras in living rooms. Home automation systems give people the capability to control their home electronic devices wherever they are.

However you need interfaces like switches and remote controls for controlling various devices in your home, interface card for your network and a router for every computer for LAN setups. Multi-zone controls, video modulators, and distribution panels for audio distributions are also used. Different devices need different hubs for setting up connections.

Home automation systems function through its major components. It includes connection center, structured wiring, and microprocessor resembling computer functions. The microprocessor let home owners operate a variety of home electronic appliances and systems wired into the connection center through touch screens, wireless keypads and remote controls through the Internet wherever you are. The home automation system's nucleus (connection center) contains the microprocessor connecting it to a series of hubs. Professional installers let the structured wiring run throughout the home to several hubs situation in a connection center.

Your home appliances and activities become free of stress through your home automation system because it provides easier management of every task. You can forecast the things before turning off your computer at the office. You will just register into the home automation system account. Turning your air conditioner on is not a problem, you just simply click an icon for the specified task. You can also determine the tasks which you have forgotten such as starting the washing machine and dishwasher through the security cameras monitor. By a click of an icon, you can start it both.

You can open the PDA (Personal Digital Assistant), while you are traveling home and got caught in traffic. By hitting a button, you can preheat your oven. Along the way, you have observed that it is already dark, the lights on the front-porch will be automatically turned on by pressing another button to welcome you when you arrived. You can use the wireless remote as you approach your neighborhood, then the home automation system will switch on the lights on your garage and opens your door, stops your security systems, and starts your pot for brewing coffee or starts playing your desired songs via your audio system.

In addition, home automation system can also perform security tasks. Basically, your home and business establishment may appear occupied but in fact, it is empty. This method is possible by setting a user timer on your television and lights. Home automation security provides well being and safety in you home giving a home or business owner peace of mind.

People can either use the hardwired or wireless security systems. Hardwired security is less expensive, however its installation can be time consuming. Also, you should have the ability in hiding wires through walls to achieve a neat installation. Now, hardwired systems can be installed using new construction methods. It provides reliability compared to its wireless counterparts.

Wireless receiver, controllers, and transmitters add to the wireless sensor's convenience. Moreover, wireless cameras could be incorporated to be more useful. Wireless security systems are easier to install and offers control flexibility. By utilizing wireless receivers and transmitters, you can place sensors easily in or out of your way or areas which are harder to access without running new wirings. Wireless systems are gaining popularity because it reduces confusing and wiring operations.

Home automation systems provide many possibilities. In recent years, it can have a speed of 100 mph and operate twenty hours a day, seven days a week. The home automation system is a tool for controlling your home devices and communication devices as well. Home automation systems eliminate tedious tasks which consumes most of the people's time. It can simplify lives. The future of home innovation will continue to cater the needs of most people worldwide.

Home Automation And The Mile-High City Of Denver

Ever since man came into existence, he has been looking for a place which he can call home. Today, the world is very much different from the way it was long ago. This is due to the intelligence of man which he used to improve his way of life. The dawn of advanced technology has brought about huge changes in man's everyday living. And it promises even more in the near future.

New technology is not only for big businesses or for organizations. You can see it working even in your own home. But the more advanced feature of it is home automation. From the word automation, you can already have a little idea of what's it all about. Automation is similar to mechanization or computerization.

At present, many huge establishments like shopping malls and banks are making use of automation. Now, the market is opening its doors to homeowners who want to incorporate home automation into their households.

In the US, home automation is no longer a new thing. If you live in Denver, Colorado, it's also easy to have home automation integrated into your present home systems.

Denver is the most heavily populated city in Colorado. It is located on High Plains and downtown Denver is just east of Cherry Creek. Denverites make up the 25th densely inhabited city in the entire US.

This 'Mile-High' city played an important role in agriculture, especially in the plains on the foot of Front Range. This city is also noted for their important contributions to the rail hub and dominance in the region of Rocky Mountains. There were even ships named after Denver. An example is the USS Denver.

Due to its connection to the systems of major transportation and its geographical position, Denver is the home of some big corporations in US. It is considered as a trade point, being located halfway between Detroit and Chicago. Distribution, as well as storage, of many services/goods is located in Denver, thereby making its economy prosper.

Home Automation Inside Out!

Government presence is considerably felt in the city because of the large number of federal agencies. Next to Washington D.C., Denver is also home to many federal workers. And this may be the reason why many state jobs are provided for Denverites.

A convention center in Colorado was completed last 2005. The expansion can attract more investors and the business sector to hold conventions in the city thereby increasing the city's earnings. The city also enjoyed economic success especially during the 70's and 80's because there was a boom in the mining sector. Silver and gold were abundant in the area that time.

Denver also allows telecommunications to take place in the north coasts, Europe, South America, and Asia in real time because of their geographic location. The city is elevated over a mile and is located at 105th meridian thereby allowing a real time 'one bounce' satellite uplink. All the six continents of the world are benefited

The economy of Denver is vulnerable to boom/bust cycles, so the state government is trying to diversify Denver's economy. The late 1990 was a period when many companies, and all of them are high tech, dominated the economy. Last 2005, the unemployment rate in the city is only 4.7% which means that a large percentage of the population are employed.

The local residents of Denver are capable of automating their homes. And this is largely based on statistics. With a high tech company in town, it's easy to find a good supplier of home automation gadgets and devices.

The city is a good target market for home automation. Since many of its residents are employed, they can afford the cool gadgets. Even the people are slowly realizing that now; having home automation around can make their lives comfortable and convenient.
If you're a Denverite, it's now time to automate. You can choose among many home automation gadgets and change your home system from its lighting, security, HVAC, and etc. to a more futuristic home.

There are many home automation companies in your locality. You can even search the internet for home automation providers. Either way, you can integrate automation into your present home system. Consult the pros and have your home done in no time.

The History Of Home Automation Inc

No organization or company will reach their peak of success without looking back to their history. They can learn a great deal about their past mistakes, and they can use it to their advantage.

Home automation is a field that is new to most people. And there are companies that supply the world with home automation devices. Since many people find home automation devices expensive, these companies are developing ways to make home automation reasonably priced so that middle class customers can afford it.

Home Automation Inc. or HAI began its operation in 1985. Their primary aim is to provide the market of automation products. HAI's founders were all from the commercial industry, they are Jay McLellan, Brian Yokum, and Tom Pickral. With their superior expertise, they concentrated their efforts to home automation.

They were able to introduce their new product in 1988, the Model 1503. It is for burglar and fire protection, appliance control, and lighting; it is a single versatile product programmable for home automation.

As years passed, their annual sales increased and now they have their own product line and their list of customers grew steadily.

From 1994 to 1999, HAI was able to offer many lines of home automation products including the Omni control system, Omnistat Communicating Thermostat, Weblink, and OmniPto control system. The president of the company then was Jay McLellan and they received the Leadership Award for Home Automation in 1999.

In the year 2000, HAI introduced to the market the control system especially designed for homes called Omni LT. They aimed at the European market and their products were for townhouses, homes, and apartments. There was a product showcase in New York that year, and they received the award as the finest new product. They also received the Choice Awards of the judges.

Web-link II was introduced by HAI in 2001. The software now has video capabilities via the media technology of Windows, wireless control and access through Internet phones, PDAs, and the homeowners are e-mailed on pre-programmed events.

Later that year, Omni II was introduced. This year is a very important one for HAI because they were able to double their warehouse size and facilities, and their sales force was expanded.

In 2002, OmniPro II was released and it replaced the first OmniPro. It was included in the top products of that same year, according to a magazine, Electronic House. Web-link II is now capable of video recording and their Omni accessories expanded because of the entry of new sensors, controllers, and mounting plates.

2003 was the year when OmniTouch was introduced. It used the touch screen interface and is very economical; and it received many awards including CES innovations Award and Achievement Award (SIA). It was regarded as part of the products which made a high impact in the market.

This year, HAI made an agreement with CompUSA, and their line of products was included in the latter's reselling program.

During 2004, new products were again introduced. They offered backlit consoles in 'cool blue', and they offered Windows software which can control the Omni family. McLellan again received an award as being included in the top 10 of the most influential leaders in the industry. They also received the Design Excellence award by ADEX.

By 2005, HAI's manufacturing facility expanded to 51,000 sq ft in New Orleans. They were able to add additional resources such as testing, training, marketing, engineering, technical support, and more warehouse space.

Hurricane Katrina damaged HAI's facility but they quickly recovered and re-opened in April 2006. This year, the company offered Omni IIe control system which can connect to the Ethernet port. They also upgraded Web-link II. HAI expanded in lighting control and they shipped 1000, 1500, 2400 watts of switches.

Last March 2006, they introduced Lumina control systems. The Lumina is a stylish lighting system which is very easy to set up in existing or new homes. You can even choose among many accessories and options.

HAI received the award 'innovator of the year' in New Orleans and McLellan won the Frost and Sullivan Award as CEO of the year in the 2006 Building Technologies.

The company has made a big name in home automation industry. It is one of the trusted suppliers of quality home automation devices all over the world.

Home Automation Jobs In Florida

The unemployment rate all over the world is quite alarming, not all countries are able to generate jobs for their local residents. This makes it difficult for ordinary people to live a decent life. And this is especially true with poor countries. But if you live in wealthy countries like the US, finding a high paying job is not very hard especially if you have good education and experience.

Living a life in Florida is not that hard. It's quite ordinary for a person to have good times, as well as bad times. But when you talk about job hunting, this is not much of a problem just as long as you're hard working.

Many of the jobs found in Florida are created by foreign companies, and it is one of the leading states in the whole US having foreign-based organizations/companies. This is called 'in-sourced jobs' while other states have jobs outsourced from overseas. This includes companies such as Siemens Corp., Medieval Times, Mitsubishi Products, Signature Flight, and Saab Training.

The local landscape of Florida is dominated by Canadian and British companies and this may be because many of the owners of these companies have been to Florida before for pleasure trips. Aside from that, there are also a majority of firms and companies coming from Germany, Japan, Australia, Finland, Brazil, France, Mexico, South Korea, Spain, and Sweden.

These companies are venturing into simulation, automation, construction, beauty shops, health services, real estate, bridal shops, aerospace, restaurants, ink printing, tourism, computer software, motor supplies, and communications.

This is also in line with President Bush's plans during his State of the Union address where he greatly stressed the generation of jobs with emphasis on science and math education, research, and physical sciences.

Most of the state's half million manufacturing jobs are now lost to automation which means that more individuals are now in the home automation business.

Home Automation Inside Out!

Home automation is not new in the market. In fact, it has been here for many years now. It is only now that more attention is given to it for the reason that the masses can now afford its products. Very few companies supply the market with home automation products. And this might be the reason why the prices of automated devices are quite expensive.

With today's shift of workers from manufacturing jobs to automation, more attention is now given to this particular sector. In due time, more people will land jobs in the automation industry. This will in turn increase the knowledge of many Florida residents about how home automation can benefit them. With more people in the automation industry, more home automation devices will be offered in the market thereby reducing their cost.

If home automation devices are more affordable, more people will purchase the devices or gadgets.

If more jobs are generated in Florida, more people will be employed. This will give then the capacity to earn income and improve their standard of living. With many people having good-paying jobs, they can now afford some luxury in life. Not that home automation gadgets are luxurious; but in due time, people will realize that it is more beneficial to have an automated home than having a traditional one.

With home automation, you can experience a life of convenience and security. If the life in Florida improves because of the increasing jobs in the market, they will be more focused in securing their homes especially when they are away. Traditional security systems are not enough. If you integrate home automation into your present security system, this will be more reliable and can give maximum protection for you and your family.

Home automation is not just about security. It can give you comfort and convenience which a traditional household can't provide. You can have automatic control over lighting, HVAC systems, pet feeding, plant watering, and so forth. This will give you more time to spend with your family and friends; you will have more time to relax and enjoy the good things in life.

So the next time that you look into the classified ads in your newspaper, look for home automation jobs. This industry promises a great deal for you as a worker and as a consumer.

How Automation Software, Automating Your House

Imagine, at exactly six in the morning, everything that you need to start your day comfortably is automatically managed. It turns on your heater to warm the house to your preference, it opens the shades in your bedroom and a soothing voice greets you good morning. As you get out of bed, the scores of the late football game you missed and the morning's headline is read out to you with that same voice and also the present day's weather forecast is included. You also noticed that as you walk toward the bathroom, the lights are automatically switched on. And, as you take a shower, your morning coffee in the kitchen is now being brewed automatically. It may sound like some kind of science fiction movie, but this technology is now widely available in the market for consumers.

Thanks to the advancement in computer technology, it is now possible to fully automate your house. Because of the hectic lifestyle that is plaguing today's people, you have to do away with all the necessary but time consuming activities to make way for more important things like work. The thought of having a computer control every aspect of your home, from turning the lights on and off to watering your lawn, you can be sure that home automation software will be able to do all this and provide you utmost convenience.

Some home automation software is included with health check systems. This works when you are looking at your bathroom mirror. On the area where you are standing, there will be sensors that will measure your height and weight. The bathroom mirror is also equipped with state-of-the-art computer technology that will remind you in text that you need to lose weight or you need to exercise.

The bathroom is also where people usually head to after waking up to do their morning routines like brushing their teeth or taking a shower before starting the day. This is why many home automation systems are emphasized widely inside the bathroom. You should also consider that with all the things you have to do as a normal person who has a job, you would need an organizer to get all the things sorted out before you start your day. With the home automation system, you can just imagine being reminded about what lies ahead during the rest of the day and what you should do, like go to meet someone, birthdays, get an oil change for your car, pick the kids up, and just about anything.

Home Automation Inside Out!

The first thing you will need is a computer to run everything. The software and sensors will be installed by a professional installer around your home. You will also be the one to pick where such sensors will be placed. The home automation software is installed in your computer and you will be the one to set your preferences. The computer together with the home automation software will be the ones that will communicate with the devices you want automated, such as lights, home security and home entertainment systems.

High end home automation includes infrared sensors and security devices to better protect your home against intruders. Some comes in digital coding devices to lock and unlock your homes and some are more sophisticated such as fingerprint recognition devices to approve entry to your house.

There are also home automation systems that come with backup power in case there is a power failure.

With home automation systems, you can ensure automated comfort and security in your home. If you have seen science fiction movies that depict future living, you will see that the future technology is now available today with home automation systems.

Today, it is now possible to live a more comfortable life with home automation systems. With the right software and the right computer, you can be sure that you and your family will be able to live in a more comfortable and secure environment. Choose a home automation system that is able to fully automate your home at your preferences.

A good home automation software program should be able to handle all your needs in your daily activities, from flicking the lights on and off, watering your lawns automatically to switching on security systems in your home, you should choose a software program that meets your automation needs.

Home Automation System, How It Works And What It Means For Your Life

People have always imagined what it would be like to live in a home where everything is automated. In fact, Hollywood made movies depicting lives in the future and show people how comfortable it would be to live in such a house. Some movies, such as iRobot and even cartoon shows, like The Jetsons, even depicted robots doing household chores and cooking fantastic dinners that can rival those of a five star restaurant chef.

Although advanced robotics technology that can do household chores and cook for your family doesn't exist yet, there are certain futuristic technology that is now widely available today. This technology is called the home automation system.

This technology is now widely available for consumers in some countries. In fact, some people today are now living in homes that you can consider as futuristic. These homes are installed with home automation systems. Although home automation systems are relatively new or is still in its infancy, it is fast becoming popular, especially to people who has a hectic lifestyle and also people with extra cash to spare for the installment of home automation systems.

First of all, you need to know how home automation systems work. Basically, there are three components that make up the home automation system. The first is the structured wiring, the second is a computer-like microprocessor and the third component is the connection center. The structured wiring is installed by professionals from where you purchased your home automation system. The wiring is installed throughout your home to the different hubs located in the connection center. The connection center is considered as the center of the home automation system and this is where all the wirings are connected. The connection center houses the microprocessor and the microprocessor is what you can consider as the brain of the whole system. This is where you program everything.

The microprocessor is responsible for allowing you to control different electronic equipments in your house, such as lights, and home electronic appliances.

Home Automation Inside Out!

The interface will be touch screens, keypads, and remote controls. Some home automation systems are connected in the internet for you to have access to it wherever you are in the world provided that you are connected to the internet.

These are the main components that make up the home automation system. The next question that many people ask is what it can do to them and how it can benefit their daily lives.

Today, people lead a very hectic lifestyle. Everything should be scheduled and people's organizers and PDA's are sometimes filled with tasks and events that may seem impossible to achieve. Many people today simply don't have enough time to do simple activities in the house. Even making coffee is now considered as an impossible task if you lead a hectic lifestyle. With home automation systems, it can make your life a bit easier to live.

If you forget turning on the dishwasher with all the dirty dishes inside, you can simply access your home automation control panel in your office and turn it on. If you forget to turn on your security system when you left your home for work, you can instantly turn it on by accessing the control panel via your PDA.

Another great thing about the home automation system is that you can preset a particular appliance or electronic equipment in your home to turn on such as your coffee maker or your home entertainment system. Just imagine, upon waking up at seven in the morning, you can expect to find freshly brewed coffee in your coffee maker. All you need to do is pour it in your coffee mug and drink. There are also home automation systems that are capable of turning off all the lights and turning on your security system inside your home automatically. This means that you no longer have to go back downstairs to check up on everything. You can simply go to bed and not worry about anything since the home automation system will take care of it.

With the home automation system, life will be easier than ever before. It can organize your life and make it stress free. Just imagine, going home at five in the afternoon, you can expect that your home air conditioning unit is turned on and your favorite music is being played in your stereo. Indeed, this particular piece of remarkable technology is now available shops near you.

Linux Home Automation Systems, Controlling Your Home Through Linux

Home automation systems are now widely available today. Even your own home computer can be installed with software and hardware devices to control your home efficiently. It may seem like science fiction, but it is now possible for you to automate your home and control all your electronic devices through your computer.

If you have the Linux software program installed, it is now possible for you to hook up all your electronic devices in it. X10 home automation systems are one of the first devices that are made compatible with the Linux software. The X10 is also one of the best known home automation devices in the world today.

First of all, you need to understand what the X10 is in order to get a better view on how it will work with your Linux software. The X10 are devices that you can plug in your electrical outlet that will allow you to control various electronic devices that is plugged in the module. There are also X10 modules that can be integrated into light switches to allow you to remotely control your lights in various rooms. Some are even installed in climate control devices for automated operation.

One great thing that the X10 developed is a device called the Firecracker. What this does is that it allows you to control all X10 devices via the serial port of your home computer. In Linux, the programs called Bottlerocket and GtkX10 will allow Linux programs to control your X10 modules with the electronic equipment plugged in via the Firecracker device.

Another great thing about this Linux add-on is that it's cheap. Only costing $5.95, you can get the Firecracker, a receiver, a lamp module, and even a remote control to operate your X10 devices.

Today, other home automation modules are now developing devices that can be attached to the PC and let you control every electronic device in your own home through the Linux program. Some companies are now making devices to be compatible to any Linux versions.

Home Automation Inside Out!

As most people know, Linux is one of the best programs ever developed to manage internet connection and act as a server. With this kind of capability, you can see that Linux is the best choice when it comes to controlling your home automation systems.

With Linux, you can control your home automation systems with a single click of the mouse. You can even install remote control programs for Linux. With this, if you are connected to the internet, you can remotely access your PC anywhere you are, provided that you have an internet connection. As you can imagine, you can control lights, and other home electronic appliances through the internet.

You can also schedule different automated features in Linux. With this capability, you will be able to schedule what time your lights will turn on and off. Imagine going home from work, and it's already seven in the evening. With the preprogrammed automation process, you can expect your lights to be switched on once you arrive home. This means additional security for your home.

You can even preprogram your stereo and your climate control device to turn on at a specific time. So, when you reach your home, you will simply enjoy your favorite music at a comfortable temperature. No longer will you have to fumble around and turn on everything that you need in order to relax. With this program and devices, your Linux can provide you with your specified relaxing atmosphere. All you need to do is sit back and relax.

If you are looking for a cheap home automation system, you can do so with various Linux program versions and add-on devices. Linux software is also required to let you gain access to various electronic equipments in your home.

As you can see, home automation can be cheap with Linux and other devices. All you need to do is get the software, get the additional hardware for your PC and install the software that can control the electronic devices in your home.

Make your life a little bit easier to live with home automation systems and a Linux program. This will change the way you live your life and many people even said that it made them live in a much more comfortable and convenient home.

Stanley Home Automation System, A Great Product For Your Everyday Needs

Mixing family and work is sometimes referred to as mixing oil and water. It just seems too impossible and many people quit their jobs in order to spend some time with their family. You also have to have some time for yourself in order to be more efficient at work. Studies have found that people who go out and have some fun, work more efficiently and happier than people who considers work as a full time activity.

You have to consider that you should get sometime for yourself and have some fun. Even for just an hour or two of doing your favorite activity, it will have positive results in your health and also in your life. This is why you should have everything in control as soon as you wake up to the moment you prepare to go to sleep.

Just imagine, at the moment you wake up, everything in your home will be prepared for you. Your coffee maker made coffee for you, and your stereo system is already playing your favorite music. It may seem like your electronic devices has a brain of its own and knows what to do to start your day. This kind of technology may seem like it's from a science fiction movie, but automatic electronic devices are now available today.

Thanks to the advancement in computer and internet technology, this is now possible through home automation systems. This particular system is perfect if you are the type of person who wants to make everything in their home run smoothly. With home automation systems, you will be able to turn on or off electronic devices in your home through a single remote control or a control panel.

With a home automation system, you can also preprogram various electronic devices in your home to operate automatically. For example, when you wake up at six in the morning, you can set your coffee maker to start brewing your morning coffee fifteen minutes before six. So, once you wake up and reach your kitchen, you can expect to have a freshly brewed coffee to be ready to start your day.

Home Automation Inside Out!

Another great thing about home automation systems is that it can be remotely operated through the internet, using your office computer or your PDA. One particular use of this system is that when you forgot to activate your home security system, and you are already in your office, you can simply access your home automation systems via a secured website online. From your office computer, you can activate your home security system.

Another example is that when you are just finishing work and is preparing to go home, you can turn on various electronic devices such as your garage lights, your living room lights, your air conditioning unit and your stereo system. Once you get home, you can expect everything that relaxes you to be turned on.

There are so many home automation systems manufacturer available in the market today. One such manufacturer is the Stanley Home Automation Systems. This particular company can offer great home automation solutions at a very competitive price.

Stanley Home Automation Systems can provide you with your automation needs. With this company, you can automate your lighting systems, your electronic garage door, your home entertainment system and even your electronic kitchen appliances.

Just imagine what you can get with Stanley Home Automation Systems. With a fully automated home, you will see that you will have more time for yourself and enjoy your life more. No more will you be burned out at work with home automation systems.

Through the Stanley Home Automation Systems, you can have a fully automated home at a very competitive price. Not only will it add more comfort and efficiency in your life, but it will give you more time to do other things that entertain you.

So, the next time you are thinking of getting a home automation system, you should consider getting Stanley Home Automation Systems. With their system, you can be sure that you will be getting great quality at a very low price. Stanley provides quality home automation systems to give you a better quality life.

Streamingmedia, Knowing The Latest News About Home Automation Systems

If you are wondering what it would be like living in a great home with all your electronic devices fully automated, such as the lights around your house, your electric oven, your microwave, your dishwasher, your home security system, and even your home entertainment system. It would be great if you can live in this kind of house where everything is controlled by a control panel which you can also program to suit your automation preferences.

Today, it is now possible for you to live in a home like this. You don't even have to move. And, if you live in an apartment, you can still have this kind of system. This automation system is called the home automation system. Just from the words itself, it may seem like it's from a Hollywood science fiction movie. However, you should consider that the future is now widely available in the market today. Although it doesn't include robots to cook great meals for you and do house chores, you should consider that technology is taking it one step closer to that possibility. And today, home automation systems are one of those technologies that you can consider installing in your own home.

Imagine this scenario. After a long day at work, you go home, prepare your dinner, eat and put the dirty dishes in the dishwasher. You then start watching a movie inside your home theatre with your large projector by activating it through your wireless control panel. You dim your lights, select a movie and sit comfortable inside and watch your favorite movie. However, you suddenly remembered that you forgot to switch on your dishwasher downstairs in the kitchen just as the movie is now starting. You don't want to get up and go downstairs again just to turn on the dishwasher and turn off the kitchen lights. What you do is take your wireless touch screen control panel beside you, touch some icons and turn on your dishwasher and turn off the kitchen lights without even standing up and leaving a comfortable position.

As you can see, home automation systems can give you the power to be in control of your own home. Another great thing about home automation systems is the capability to preprogram your electronic devices. Upon waking up in the morning, you are greeted good morning by a soothing voice. Your window blinds automatically open up to reveal a great day ahead of you. As you go downstairs to your study room, you see a list of the activities you have to do that is already neatly printed for you to review. As you review your schedule, and make your way to your kitchen, you see a freshly brewed coffee ready for you. All you need to do is pour some coffee in your mug and listen to the same soothing voice reading the weather forecast and news headlines for you.

Things like this can make your life a little bit easier for you to live. Because most of these systems are already connected to the internet, you can access your home automation systems via the internet even if you're not home. This means that you can check your home once in a while. This is also very useful when you are already inside your office and forgot about turning on your burglar alarm system. For most people, this can make a good day turn into a complete mess. With home automation systems, you don't need to worry about it ever again. All you need to do is access your system through the internet and turn on the burglar alarm system remotely.

If you want more information about home automation system, you will know about it in Streamingmedia by visiting their website at www.streamingmedia.com. Through this website, you will see real-time streaming about the latest home automation systems available. You can even see a specific system at work or a demonstration. With this kind of website, you can indeed determine which home automation system you should purchase.

So, if you are looking for a home automation system, the best way to determine which kind of home automation will suit your needs is through Streamingmedia. Here, you will find out about the different kinds of home automation systems available and watch it in action. You can also read reviews and know which system have satisfied a lot of customers. Through Streamingmedia, you can be sure that you will know about the latest technology in the home automation industry.

Wireless Home Automation, What This Means For Your Daily Life

In order to get your day to start running smoothly, you have to start improving your life in your home. Today, the way people do their daily rituals in their homes have become somewhat of a challenge. This is because of the hectic lifestyle in modern society that people are currently living in. One way to start making your daily routines in your home to be much easier than ever before is to install a home automation system.

It may sound like it came out of a science fiction television show but home automation systems are now widely available for consumers today. With this system, you will be able to control your home wherever you are. A single touch screen control panel or a remote control will be your tool to communicate with every electronic device found in your home.

Home automation today is very popular to a lot of people. With home automation, you can live life the easier and more comfortable way. There are so many benefits that home automation systems can give you. However, most home automation systems today require a structured wiring in order for it to work and communicate with your control panel. This can be very inconvenient especially if it means taking the walls apart in your home for the structured wiring and putting it back again to conceal it.

This can take a lot of time to do especially if you have a rather large home. One way to get rid of this step is to get a wireless solution for home automation systems. This will only require you to change the electrical outlet and the light switch. The special electrical outlet where you will plug your electronic devices in your home, such as your home security systems, your home entertainment system, your air conditioning unit, and also your coffee maker, is integrated with an RF transceiver. The same goes for the special light switches. This means that the wiring will never be changed. Another addition is a special remote control or a wireless touch screen control panel with a charger. This will be your communications device to all the electronic devices plugged in your special electronic outlet.

Some wireless home automation systems are just plug in adaptors with RF transceivers. The only downside of wireless home automation systems is that the devices that will be integrated around your home will cost a lot more than wired home automation systems. However, when you think about it, it is much more convenient that wired home automation systems. With this, you will be able to switch any electronic device on even when you are not really physically in the area where the switch is located. All you need to do is communicate with the specific device using the wireless control panel. So, if you are already in your bedroom and you are preparing to get some shut eye, and you suddenly remembered that the light is on in your den on in any part of your house that you need to turn off, you can simply access it through your wireless control panel and switch it off.

Also, if you want coffee made after you take a shower, you can turn your coffee maker on before you take a shower. Once you get to the kitchen after showering, you can expect a freshly brewed coffee already made.

Some wireless home automation systems are now connected to the internet and are also integrated with home security systems, such as CCTV security cameras and alarm systems. These can also be activated and deactivated through the control panel or through the internet. This means that even if you're not at home, you can control various electronic devices inside your home through a secured website.

So, if you are planning to get the best kind of home automation systems or if you want a home automation system that is more convenient than your existing one, you should consider getting a wireless home automation system. This system will be able to give maximum control to your home.

Always remember that you should first ask your family and friends on what kind of wireless home automation system you should purchase. Another great way to find out about the best kind of home automation system is by looking at the reviews. Indeed, wireless home automation system can definitely give you the additional comfort and convenience you need when you live life in the fast lane.

The Home Automation Code

Safety is something that millions of people across the world desire for their homes. One of the major reasons for this is due to the amount of time spent within the home. From the early morning coffee to the late night shower, millions of people spend the majority of their lives in their home, and, as such, they also desire to spend it under the safest conditions possible. Safety is one of the foremost thoughts in everyone's mind, that is, right after comfort.

Since living in comfort is everyone's top priority, we see home owners and renters spending hundreds of dollars just one simply luxuries that have no practical value. Many of the examples of this are the surround sound system that is linked with the entertainment center, or the computer connected to the fasted internet connection possible.

When you think of Home Automation, immediately something out of Star Trek comes to mind. Even though it does, in fact, sound like something straight out of science fiction, this is not a "years to come" device. Many people all over the world have these Home Automation Systems, and not one of them has brought it with them from a distant future.

The future, as far as Home Automation is concerned, crashed landed in the mid 1980's with the establishing of Home Automation, Inc. Revolutionary for its time, the products that this company began to release brought a whole new level of safety, security and luxury unlike any previous generation has known. As their company began to grow, so did their reputation and their ingenuity. It was not before long until they started whole lines of products that everyone just had to have.

As you consider which provider you should choose to purchase and have your automation system installed from, Home Automation, Inc. is one of your more professional and more helpful choices. They bring a level of professionalism to their work that is unheard of in their industry, not to mention their ability to continuously satisfy their customers.

What, you might ask, would this automation system offer me? Well, to say the least, it will offer the convenient control of your entire home from your chair in the living room. Yes. Once installed, you will be able to do everything from secure the premises with your alarm system to adjusting the room's temperature.

Allow us to paint a picture of what your normal morning would be like with your new automation system. Let's say you wake up early and you have a meeting in two hours. You rise from your slumber and hit a few buttons on your wireless controller by your bed. You hop in your shower and try to wake up. By the time you enter your kitchen, the coffee has just stopped brewing and the music you enjoy listening to before you head off to work is playing softly from the radio in the Living Room. This would be just a few of the major benefits given from this automation system.

Another fantastic benefit offered by this system is immediate convenience. Let's say you just pull into your garage after a long day. As you pull in, you dread the thought of fumbling in your pockets for your keys. Just as you think about that, the lights kick on from the sensors in the garage. Your driveway and your living room are now luminous and welcoming you back home.

Yet another major benefit you receive from this system is not something you can see, but rather something many other people will see. By simply setting the system on random, you can have your house lit periodically while you are on an extensive vacation, as to conceal your absence from prying eyes. This is just a portion of the safety devices available to home owners. With this new system, an extra sense of danger is given to those who desire your hard earned possessions. You can even have your music set to play in the evenings, as you would normally like to do.

But the benefits of long travel security don't end there. If you have access to a computer with a connection to the internet, you can view your home's cameras remotely. Yes. Since most of the equipment from Home Automation is setup with CCTV cameras, all that is left is for you to have a connection in your home, and you will have instant access to your home's security from anywhere on the planet.

With all of this new technology, it is easy to get caught up in the risk factor of intelligent hackers. This is why the automation system comes with security codes, which make it nearly impossible for intruders to break.

Home Automation Inside Out!

After reading this article, we hope that getting a home automation system has become one of the top priorities on your home improvement lists. Getting these benefits and more from Home Automation, Inc. is just a beginning. By installing this system, you will greatly increase your sense of comfort, security, and peace of mind while enjoying the confines of your own home.

Home Automation Gear

Home automation or home mechanization is the most extensively attained system all through the country. The popularity it has gained is mainly due to the innumerable advantages which it offers to its users.

Home mechanization system has been evolving rapidly in many forms for some years now. From the uncomplicated intruder alarm to the more complex mechanization of multimedia appliances, this surely deserves to be referred to as one of the very innovative ideas which the world has come across.

Any kind of electronically or electrically powered device or appliance can make use of the home mechanization system. The main idea behind the whole process is to make control all manually operated appliances in a programmed manner under any given situation.

Prior to this system being used in homes, this was used significantly in big offices and huge buildings. The main difference between home automation and building automation is that the former is very simple while the latter is quite complex. It becomes easy to maneuver many appliances when the mechanization system is employed in big structures.

Almost all electronic appliances at home can be mechanized. Beginning from the lighting and heating system to the safety alarm, everything can be automated. In the current era, this mechanization system can also be used for electrical machines, televisions and other components.

Home mechanization can be wireless. In case of buildings under construction, permanent wires may be fixed to the walls and can then be connected to chief controller. Wireless mechanization is the best option when it comes to houses where it is not possible to fix wires.

Home Automation Inside Out!

Home mechanization has grown into a huge field now and there are specialists available to take care of all your home automation problems and provide solutions. They can be sought through the internet or otherwise.

Given below is the list of the most frequently automated equipments at home:

1. Audio

The most commonly mechanized device is the audio system. Conventionally, audio systems are always positioned at a fixed place in the house which is often the function room or the living room. Such devices can be automated in such a way that one can listen to music at any given time without disturbing the others by placing and connecting the speakers accordingly. Inversely, all the members can listen to music at the same time if needed. This is referred to as multi-zone audio system.

2. HVAC

HVAC can be elaborated as Heating, Ventilation, and Air Conditioning. It is also referred to as climate control. In case, refrigeration is also included in this mechanization system, it would be termed HVAC+R. all the appliances in this process can be automated by using several schemes. Once this system is adopted, it is not necessary to maneuver the appliances for setting the temperature, humidity and other related factors. For instance, the air conditioner can be automated in such a way that it switches on once the room temperature reaches a certain level. The same technique can be used for all the other appliances which are contained in the HVAC+R system.

3. Intercom

This is an electronically operated communication device which is used for local purposes. The working of an intercom is similar to the working of a telephone. However, its operation is confined to the building or its location. It is used in homes to communicate between rooms. Automation of the intercom will facilitate features such as two ways or three way calling.

4. Lighting

Lighting systems are maneuvered in almost all the cases as it comprises of only two steps namely OFF and ON. However, even this system can be mechanized to perform the required task at the stipulated time. For instance, the lighting system can be automated to switch on at a certain time every day and to switch off after a particular period of time as dawn strikes. The system can also be mechanized according to the brightness needed at different times of the day. This is programmed in such a way that once the room occupancy is exceeded after a particular level, the lighting system would automatically increase the brightness.

There are more such home appliances which can be mechanized according to our wants and needs.

Do-it-Yourself Home Automation Projects

There are so many things which can be done to automate your appliances without the help of a specialist. These simple techniques do not need you to take any special care or supervision.

With the level of technology that is prevalent today, home mechanization is surely not an impossible thing to do. Home mechanization is the best solution if you are ready to face the brunt for owning a high-tech home.

Mechanization of your house is not a very difficult task to do. It is not really necessary for you to use gadgets that are complex. You can rather settle with simple gadgets for the easy-to-do home mechanization program. The X10 is one amazing example of one such easy to use gadget and this belongs to the DIY range.

The first constraint to your project would always be your budget. Every home mechanization project that you undertake, whether big or small, requires you to set some budget apart for it. Determining the budget required for a home automation project is not a very easy thing to do as you may not be familiar to the whole concept.

It is very necessary to make out the things which you are planning to integrate in your mechanization project. You need to select the particular thing or things according to your plan and requirements. As the project involves you to take care of many things such as lighting, monitoring controls for HVAC+R, security devices and other similar devices which you are planning to control, you will have to divide your work accordingly. You can divide it according to the task to be performed or as per the room you are planning to automate.

When proceeding with room automation, again, it is necessary to decide on the devices to be automated and their order. You can decide the order of mechanization of draperies, lights, security systems, fans and appliances as per your requirements and convenience. You need to prepare separate lists for the problems which you may have to face, the budget and the particular devices which would be needed.

Home Automation Inside Out!

You can automate your house according to tasks if you are planning to do all the work by yourself. Under such a circumstance, it is totally up to you to decide the order of mechanization. You can start up with the lights or the fans, the security systems or the HVAC etc. You can start according to your convenience and requirement and proceed with the work fittingly.

There are endless options available once you have decided to proceed with your home mechanization plan. The fundamental mechanization kit would not cost you more than $30. It is important for you to prepare the budget once you have decided the devices and appliances which you are going to mechanize.

Soon after making your budget, you can start purchasing the necessary tools. You can choose from a wide range of products belonging to different brands. If you feel that the expensive products are worth the price, go for them. Otherwise, you can stick to the cheaper ones which would serve your purpose. This feature applies especially if you are working under a limited budget.

If you are ready to experiment with stuff you can try using more resourceful and handy products. However, for this you should be ready to burn a hole in your pocket. For example, if you are falling short of electrical outlets at your house, you can go in for 3-prong modules which may be used along with pass-through connectors. And in case of X10 projects, you will have to follow this option.

If you are going with an X10, you will have to choose all the necessary frills or accessories for your project to turn out well. You would need screwdrivers, both straight and head, spare batteries, voltage sensors, so on and so forth.

If you are planning to go ahead with the lighting system, you need to identify the lighting requirements according to the different rooms. You can also do it according to the likes and preferences of your people. A brighter lighting for the study, dining room and drawing room and a dimmer one for the bedrooms is preferable.

You can take the help of your people if you are not fine with doing all the work by yourself. This would also make the work more enjoyable and fun. Once the work is done, you will feel great about it and so will your family.

GE Products For Home Automation Security And Protection

There is a huge variety of merchandise available in the market which you can go for while planning mechanization of the security systems at your house. You need to choose the correct brand according to your requirement. You need to pick the correct brand after careful examination and thought.

Home mechanization is not a new field. It has been in existence for some years now. Many movies have already brought forward the concept of home automation. It has become quite a rage of late. These techniques, which are quite simple when professional help is taken, can make your residence a more comfortable, safer and better place to be in.

Home can truly give your family a whole new experience. With the home mechanization system installed, you can catch up with movies with all the effects with your audio video system; you can also create the perfect ambience by setting up the lighting system accordingly. After the movie, you can hit the bed without having any fear as the system would turn on the security devices and all doors and windows will also be checked and locked. Such attributes lessen your tension to a great extent.

There is a huge range of security devices for you to choose from to secure your house from all sorts of problems. DSC, GE, Visonic, Sensaphone, Optex, Winland and Sky Link to name a few, are the major brands. These security systems will guarantee your home to be secured under any circumstance.

The GE range of products has a huge collection of specially designed gadgets for security purposes. Its intrusion device is one major example. The brand has always provided its customers with quality products and has a large base of trusting customers.

Given below is the list of the security products coming from GE:-

1. The wireless Home Security System (80-307-3X-GE Simon3) is a highly improved security system which is sleek and wireless and is also stylish.

Home Automation Inside Out!

2. Alphanumeric Touchpad (60-983 ATP1000) is a device with built in speakers helps you perform a variety of functions. It helps you control the activation, operation and programming of your house security system. It has alarms for the police, fire and other panic buttons which you can make use of in case of emergency.

3. Hardwire or Wireless Kit (80-871 GE Concord) is a system which is very useful for burglary and fire detection. It comprises of window sensors, motion sensors, LCD touchpad, crystal door sensors, and an interior speaker.

4. Allegro Wireless Security System (80-795-GE) is a security system is an add-on to the security systems belonging to the family of Interlogix. It is a very economical one.

5. Fast pack Alarm System Kit (NX-4-FP-GE Security) is one of the most convenient and cost-efficient security systems. It has all basic options.

All the above mentioned products are just few of the best selling ones. There is a huge collection of many more advanced and popular security systems from GE which you can check out by logging on to many websites. More comprehensive search can be made by logging on to the official website of GE electronics.

Home automation has contributed to a great deal in making many families feel secured. It has provided solutions for a safer and more convenient place to stay in and enjoy. The benefits of home mechanization cannot be listed out very easily as there are lots of advantages of this system in almost every sphere of your house. GE is the most preferred name when it comes to home mechanization. The reason behind this is that they offer a wide variety of products to suit your every need. You can either opt for their whole range of security systems or can go in for individual products.

GE has every variety of products to secure your house and your possessions so that the place is totally secured and you can proudly call it your home than just your house! The website of GE has the list of all the products available, their features and working. You can check that out and decide what product to opt for. So, why waste more time? Simply log on to the GE website and choose the products needed as per your budget and requirements.

Home Automation And GE Products For Excellent Lighting And Security

Performance of a person can be affected to perform any given task under certain circumstances like their capability, mood and health. One of the above factors are lighting, only in the recent times peoples are coming to know the importance of lighting, are the various benefits attached to it. When the user finds a home with very good lighting attached to it, then he/ she are placed in a positive environment, where they could take some quick and right decisions in no time, due to the positive energy flows through. But this whole concept is not been realized by the owners or they can be even said that they are unaware of this whole fact.

Generally, the owners or the person who live in a house use a 60 watt power tube light bulb for their use. These tube light bulbs can be used in the user's room too. The light system what we are using currently can cause you up to twenty percent of your house hold bills, where the performance of it so poor that it can be used even for using both heating and lighting. Halogen tube bulbs which are used for certain house hold purposes can produce more heat than that of lighting.

Due to the advancement and up gradation of technology, and home automation, technologists have developed a new type of tube bulb, which provides better lighting and heat with a very low cost. By upgrading this latest technology, GE has turned out to be world leaders in this field of manufacturing tube bulbs. GE is a well known tube light manufacturing brand which provides a very high quality products and services that produces convenience and comforts to the millions of users around the world.

GE's new technology provides great ambience to your home that brings life into the millions of houses which are carefully selected and cautiously done. BY making better lighting surroundings at home it gives a great comfort and life to the family member's joy and provides a warmth atmosphere. There are plenty of ways to use the GE lighting products in your home that suits you and everybody's life style.

Home Automation Inside Out!

GE technology lightening offers you a various great services halogen bulbs, incandescent bulbs, linear fluorescent and compact and other newly developed enrich bulbs from GE. These newly enrich bulbs are basically designed to fit the various rooms situated in your house.

Let's start explaining it in detail from living room. This one is the most sought after and the most used room of the lot, this has to suit various situations and activities, and come out pleasing to suit all these needs. Hence this above use , one can use GE halogen linear tube bulbs as the rays of this light falls on the ceiling and thus makes it vibrant and brightens the room color and helps to make the living room more appealing. One can attach more touches with the lightening shades to your room with the various GE enrich products such as Softlight, Halo GLS, Biax Extra Mini and Enrich Reflectors.

Next let us look up to the dinning room, which as to be the most pleasing of it, where to both the family members and the guest who attend there house. Meanwhile, you might invite sometime your friends to the party, where the owner has to remember that the dinning room has to be romantic and pleasing for the guests who attend it as well. If you need to create such kind of ambience to the guest who arrive to your home then it is always advisable to use GE enrich Candle, Decor Candle, or the Biax Extra Mini. The owner can add up on dimmer switches so that it creates friendly and intimate atmosphere for the users.

Advantages Of Home Automation Systems

In this century, world has turned so faster that taking care of their own home itself is so difficult and not possibly effectively. The few peoples who has time as mobbed down due to this routine work and they have turned tired of doing the same work time and again. One has to remember and accept to the fact that in today's faster world people really do not have time to spend for themselves and enjoy their leisure activities.

That is the reason for peoples of this era trying to save those precious times to their leisure activities by installing those home automation products in their house and trying to have some fun. You might think that this whole concept is a typical Hollywood commercial which is not available but it is not true, this whole concept is currently available in market and doing wonders for its users.

We have to thank to the advancement of technology and the inventions of this home automation, which was once considered as the typical Hollywood saga has turned out to be a big boon and helping all its users across the globe. Although this whole technology looks like something fantasy happening around us, it is catching very quicker as days passes on and provides a time saver mainly for those peoples who are involved in the hectic life style as it eases their pressure. But the user has to remember, since the whole technology runs in the computer with state- of - art technology, we need to shell out some more money, as it worthy of it.

When the user has money and wants to make life simpler and ready to shell out money from their pocket, and then straight away head to home automation. With the facilities and advantages of the home automation is been endless, one can expect the growth of this industry in a rapid rate with as high as possible. One could ever imagine have a single remote control to access the entire home and advantages of using it is unexplainable. It would so easy and convenient and will also easy the pressure of the hectic day of the users.

By bringing this technology, one can say relation between fictions and reality continues. Because of the competition there are lots of latest and various home automation systems available in the market. By this various ranges now available, one can easily pick out the ones required and the one that suits them best for all their needs up. One must also make sure that he picks the one that really suits all his needs and works for it.

First of all the user needs to know what it all takes to use the home automation and how it works, because without it one can never define what works good for him and the comfort it gets them. It is basically defined into three different categories, which are named as just like in a computer such as connection center, microprocessor and structured wiring. These complete wiring structures is been designed by the company whom they design this home automation, by the professionals they hire. The wiring system works by passing through all your electronic equipments which need to be automated such as home entertainment system, lights and kitchen appliances.

These whole wiring structures passes through the main connection centre, which is the micro processor. This work of technology is said to be the home automation, which is been practiced and installed in their home.

Home Automation Through Voice Recognition Systems

If you ever wondered of accessing your complete home through a single control panel, just like the way it happens in the Hollywood flicks then you need not dream more, it has finally arrived to fulfill your dreams. Because of advancement in technology, this whole concept has turned into reality and came into existence. To be perfect the future technologies what we see in the Hollywood flicks, have came into existence, thanks to this home automation technology.

In the past peoples have used this home automation system, in their business to ease their work. Even though this technology came in the past, it was too costly, to be installed in the homes. But as days passes on these technology has turned very cheap, where some of the leading companies with a competitive price and provides a great service for the users.

Due to the high demand and requirements from the users, this home automation industry have turned out to be a big hit, which forwards the number, of new organization branching into it. By this increase in number of companies and turning to be highly competitive, the prices of home automation have come down considerably. The installer and manufacturers have come straight to the private consumers and boosting them to install this home automation system right in their home.

Users have to remember one thing, installing home automation does not mean just a luxury, and it also gives you better chance to have a convenient and better lifestyle and gives you more time to relax. With arrival of this new technology and the advancement of it, the user need not worry about losing their valuable time in taking care of their home and spend it to ease them off.

It is basically defined into three different categories, which are named as just like in a computer such as connection center, microprocessor and structured wiring. These complete wiring structures is been designed by the company whom they design this home automation, by the professionals they hire. The wiring system works by passing through all your electronic equipments which need to be automated such as home entertainment system, lights and kitchen appliances.

These whole wiring structures passes through the main connection centre, which is the micro processor. This work of technology is said to be the home automation, which is been practiced and installed in their home.

Let us now look about voice recognition in home automation. This piece of technology has added a great deal to the current home automation concept and results have come up to great deal and the manufactures have added it to their packages. With this piece of voice recognition technology in you home automation, one can easily switch on and switch off their home appliances, with just a mere sound of your voice.

For instance, if you find struggling to search for light switches or the control panel in the night in your bedroom, one can easily access to it by their voice recognition by saying what they have assigned for that.

That is the reason for peoples of this era trying to save those precious times to their leisure activities by installing those home automation products in their house and trying to have some fun. You might think that this whole concept is a typical Hollywood commercial which is not available but it is not true, this whole concept is currently available in market and doing wonders for its users.

Home Automation For Light Control

Are you one among those who tend to mess up stuff at the middle of the night while trying to find switch on the bathroom light? If so, home mechanization can provide great solutions or you. Every electronic appliance can be controlled by this means than merely the lighting system.

Home mechanization has created a lot of buzz and has rapidly grown into a fast developing field. The added advantage is that it is affordable and is also easily available. It has become a fad in the United States of America. This system makes life easy and simple and helps home owners in saving time in a variety of ways. The hype it has created has made many people conclude that home automation is a very wise way of investing money on your house. Many people have started mechanizing their houses so that they do not have to maneuver with the appliances all the time.

People have started believing that installing a home mechanization system at their homes would enhance their standard of life. Many people have become ready to burn a hole in their pockets by installing state-of-art home mechanization systems at their houses according to the latest technological up gradation. You can operate the electronic appliances at your house from anywhere with this mechanization system.

Home automation has advanced to such a great extent that you can operate your appliances sitting in the office or even when you are on a vacation. All it takes is to log on to the particular secured website and control your home mechanization system. You can operate all your appliances and can also switch on and off lights whenever needed.
And this has its own share of advantages when it comes to impressing your loved ones.

You can set the brightness of the lights differently from room to room according to your needs and preferences. For instance, you can create a really romantic ambience by dimming the lights in your house by just using your PDA. You can set it up before you bring back your loved one home after an awesome twosome dinner. Hence, you are saved of the embarrassment of looking for switches at the middle of the night.

Home Automation Inside Out!

You can also opt for timing your lighting devices. It can be done by setting a timer for the lights to switch on or off at a particular time everyday. By this means, you can make sure that the pathway and porch lights are shining bright when you go home after a tiring day's work.

Many mechanization systems can also be operated with a control panel which is wireless. With the help of such a control panel, you can switch off the kitchen light even without taking the effort of getting out of your bed. You can easily switch off any light using the touch screen control panel from anywhere around the house.

This mechanization system also offers a great scope for protecting your house from burglars. While going on a vacation or when no one is around, you can time the lighting devices in such a way that it makes it seem as if someone is home.

One great way in which the advancement in technology has been helpful is that you do not have to change the wiring system in your entire house. Instead, all it takes is connecting the existing wires with a radio frequency which would help in controlling the lighting system by way of RF communication. You just have to install the radio frequency communication equipment. This would also ensure convenience and efficiency as the existing wiring at your house will remain untouched.

Home mechanization is a boon in many ways. It helps in controlling the electronic appliances at your house from anywhere. Lighting systems can be controlled from any place even if you are on a vacation with your family. An added benefit is the internet which helps in communicating with the automation system at your place from anywhere at anytime of the day.

So, if you are planning to make an investment on your house, make it by way of home mechanization systems. Opt for the best protocols in the mechanization network for increased efficiency and convenience.

Security CHS 400 Home Automation System

By the amount of crime rate increasing day to day, security has turned out to be big cause of concern for the house owners. Homes which are considered as safe as heaven now have turned vulnerable due to the thieves trespassing into the houses. For the above reasons leaving a home alone as turned out to be a big cause of concern for the house owners and thus they try to avoid there long journey too.

If one needs to get free from the above things, then it is always better to protect their house by a very good security system. With the above technology of Security CHS 400 Home Automation System, One can be sure of the thing that their house is completely safe and no intruders could get into their house for sure.

But before happening to it, one should think of which exactly the security the have plan to install. It has to be good enough to save it from the intruders. Today there are lots options available in the market and one should think twice before choosing the right one that suits their family needs. The user should not face hesitant to shell out more money when it comes to his security. It comes as the priority when compared to that of the cost.

Indeed, home automation systems can definitely bring comfort and convenience to anyone who has one. Even your coffee maker and your dishwasher can be automated through this system. If you want a freshly brewed coffee at the time you wake up, you can expect it to be ready by then with home automation system. All you have to do is pour it in your coffee mug and drink it.

Control panels can also be placed anywhere you wish to place it. You can have a control panel in your bedroom, and you can also have a separate control panel in your living room. In fact, there are available wireless touch screen control panels that are now widely available in the market today. With home automation systems, you can have the ability to control everything at a touch of an icon in your control panel screen.

This will give you a demonstration on how home automation works and how it can make your life easier and much more convenient to live.

Home Automation Inside Out!

So, whenever you are going shopping for a home automation system, you can just log in to the internet and look for streaming media about home automation systems. Usually, you will find these at home automation systems manufacturer's websites or at technology websites. The streaming media will provide you a closer look at what home automation is all about and also determine which system is best for you.

If you still can't imagine what it would be like to live in a home like this, you can take a look at streaming media in various website that features home automation systems. Some home automation systems manufacturer are now including streaming media in their website to provide a much better view for you to determine what home automation systems is all about.

With the streaming media in the internet about home automation systems, you will be able to know about living in a future home. The best thing about this is that your existing home can be installed with home automation systems. The streaming media will provide you a closer look on how the system is installed and how you can benefit from it. Some are in the Macromedia Flash format where you can interact with the home automation system.

Streaming Media In Home Automation

The wiring will then go to the connection center which houses the microprocessor. This is the core of the home automated system and this is where everything in your home is controlled. The interface will consist of touch screen control panels, a remote control and some home automated systems that are connected to the internet where you can gain access to the control panel via the internet.

Just imagine you forgot about turning on your home security systems and you are on your way to work, all you have to do is access the control panel through your PDA or in the office computer that is surfing to the internet. Because of this, you will no longer worry about the security of your home.

Another great thing about it is that before you reach your home, everything will be prepared for your convenience. At your specification and customization of the automated process, you can program it to start playing your favorite music, or start the air conditioning or heating unit in a specific time, before you reach home.

There are also home automated systems that are voice activated. If you are having a hard time finding the switches for the lights, you can easily turn it on through your own voice.

For example, if you find yourself fumbling around a dark bedroom and are having trouble finding the switches or control panel, you can easily ask for lights by saying what you specified in the voice module on what speech pattern it should recognize to turn on the lights. After climbing in to bed and you are already comfortable, one can easily turn the lights off again with your voice through the same process.

The first thing you have to do is specify what you will say to turn on a specific device. For example, you can program the voice recognition module to turn on the lights after it hears you say "lights on" and turning off the lights when you say "lights off".

Home Automation Inside Out!

You can also use voice recognition modules in your stereos or your home entertainment systems. You can even install it in your kitchen electronic appliances. All one need to do is program it to recognize your voice and the specific command.

It is very important that you should really think about which home security system that you should purchase. It should be able to function and effectively deter intruders. Today, there are different home security products available in the market. You should consider getting a home security system that suits your family's needs. No matter what the cost is, you should consider the fact that the safety of your family is priceless.

One kind of home security product is the Security CHS Home Automated System. Not only that this product is a security system, but it is also a home automation system in one package. The great thing about this product is the home automation capability. With this kind of capability, you can have additional protection rather than just alarms and automatic emergency calls to alert the proper authorities.

If you want to live a futuristic home, all you have to do is install a home automated system with a voice recognition system. With it, you can live life as if you are in the future.

The Security CHS Home Automated System is also capable of controlling every piece of electronic equipment inside your home. It can control you entertainment system, your lights, your home security system and even your coffee maker. With this benefit, you can control every part of your home at the palm of your hands.

Avenues Of Home Automation - Future Living, An Insight

In the rapid pace with which the world is advancing today, almost everyone is opting for home mechanization systems. This is mainly due to the fact that even a small anomaly in your schedule can ruin the whole day's work. For instance, a problem in your security system when you are in a great hurry to go to office might make you lose your concentration the whole day. This would result in your mood being spoilt to a great extend and may also lead to unnecessary tension.

A smooth start to a day would ensure a great day while a hitch early in the morning would ruin it all. You cannot possibly go back home and get the security system corrected right away as it would ruin all your other schedules for the day.

Home automation makes it presence felt in all such situations. It provides solutions for an easier and more convenient way of life. Many people have even confirmed that installing a home mechanization system has resulted in them being less tensed and has thus decreased stress levels to a great extent. The system ensures that people are free from the woes of taking care of their appliances and all other electronic devices at home when they are busy getting ready to do their work.

Home mechanization system provides you with a lot of advantages. An illustration to help you understand this point better is that if you have forgotten to activate your security system, you can do so by activating it from your office by accessing it through your PDA or through the internet by means of a secured website.

This lessens your worries and makes life easy for you. Controlling the home mechanization system through the internet is just one of the many advantages of the system. The next big benefit of this system is that it helps you in preprogramming your appliances in such a way that they get switched on automatically as per the requirement.

For example, if you rise at six in the morning to get ready for work, your automated appliances can help you in every way possible. The window blinds would automatically rise revealing the beautiful day ahead for you. Secondly, the bathroom lights shine bright and the state-of-art mirror in the bathroom may even display your height and weight and even the weather forecast for the day. Your itinerary for the day lie printed over the printer and by the time you head down for breakfast, your favorite freshly brewed coffee would be ready and waiting for you.

It should be noted that once you mechanize your appliances as per your needs, all the work that ought to be done like preparing coffee to printing your schedule for the day would be done automatically.

One of the major confusions which you will have to face is deciding the brand to opt for while shopping for home mechanization systems. Every manufacturer would claim to be the best. In order to choose the best as per your needs, all you need to do is to check out the website of the various manufacturers and their products for more comprehensive knowledge about it and then choose the one which you think would be the best. You can also check out the working of the systems by taking a look at the various videos posted in the web sites.

The best way to choose the home mechanization system to be purchases is by taking a look at the working of various systems with the help of streaming media provided in the websites. Once you are sure about the working of a particular product, you can decide whether to go for it or to check out better products.

This Product Is Brought To You By